MINDFULNESS MODERATES IMPULSIVITY AND ALCOHOL

SARAH HOCHBERG

Abstract

In active addiction, the brain's neural systems orient towards satisfying cravings to reduce biomechanical stress, by boosting craving and reward signals and inhibiting decision-making in the prefrontal cortex. This stands as a risk factor for drinking-related consequences. Mindfulness, with its features of intentional awareness and present-moment focus, can aid with the reduction of impulsivity, and decrease those consequences. In this study, participants completed self-report questionnaires for impulsivity, mindfulness, and drinking-related consequences. Correlations were analyzed, and eight mediational models were run, utilizing subscales and facets of the constructs. Mindfulness facets (Observing, Nonreactivity, Acting with Awareness, Nonjudging) acted as either full or partial mediators to attenuate the effects of impulsivity on increased drinking problems. Mindfulness skills could enhance one's ability to learn to act differently across situations, disrupting trait-based impulsivity with interventions tailored towards

interrupting the reward and sensation-seeking behaviors that can lead to negative consequences.

Table of Contents

List of Tables

Table	Page

The Mediating Effect of Mindfulness on Impulsivity, with regards to Alcohol Use

Chapter I: Introduction

Statement of the Problem

From workplace functions at happy hours to bottomless mimosas at brunch, alcohol misuse has become normalized throughout society. This is not in and of itself problematic but can certainly pave the way for unintentional use and ensuing issues stemming from dependency. In 2019, 26% of people surveyed ages 18 and older reported that in the past month, they had engaged in binge drinking, and 6% reported heavy alcohol use (National Institute on Alcohol Abuse and Alcoholism [NIAAA], 2019). It is well-documented that excessive alcohol use can cause serious physical harm, such as cirrhosis of the liver, fibrosis, alcohol hepatitis, cancer, cardiovascular disease, and anemia (NIAAA, 2018). Further, in terms of brain chemistry, alcohol use and ensuing hangovers have been linked to the loss of overall brain matter and shrinkage of total brain size, greater deficits in the frontal superior cortex, and loss of white matter in the frontal lobe (Sullivan et al., 2010).

One of the ways alcohol addiction works on a biomechanical level is it inhibits the prefrontal cortex (PFC) and over-engages the striatal-limbic and dopaminergic pathways. The PFC is in charge of executive functioning. This entails risk assessment, risk management, and accordant decision-making. Substance use dampens the body's decision-making processes, increasing risky impulsivity, and over-seeks sensation and reward chemicals. Addiction occurs when the body's natural evolutionary survival mechanisms of neural adaptation develop tolerance, requiring more of a substance to achieve the same effect. Without the homeostasis achieved only through regular and increased use, withdrawal occurs, which could

5   involve emotional dysregulation, fatigue, muscle pain, nausea, and even seizures

(West & Gossop,

1994). This cycle of intake, tolerance, withdrawal, and increased intake continues onward, leading to greater interpersonal and intrapersonal distress and significantly worsening consequences.

Purpose of the Study

Research has shown that increased impulsivity can be a risk factor for increased drinkingrelated consequences (Park et al., 2014). A PFC with dampened responsiveness due to alcohol use is primed for risky decision-making. Mindfulness has a focus on present moment and intentional heightened awareness, which past research has shown can decrease impulsivity (Bowirrat & Oscar-Berman, 2005). This study aims to discover if mindfulness has a mediating effect on impulsivity, and if this effect yields lowered drinking-related consequences.

Research Question and Hypotheses

One hypothesis in the study was that higher levels of impulsivity would be associated with increased drinking-related behaviors. An additional hypothesis to the study was that higher mindfulness scores would be associated with lowered impulsivity, which would act as a mediating variable and result in lowered drinking-related consequences.

Chapter II: Review of the Literature

Mechanisms of Addiction

In a wild oversimplification of the factors leading to addiction, drugs feel good. To use a push-pull paradigm, substances often serve the purpose of pushing away from negative affect and pulling towards a feeling of escape in some capacity. Relief

6   is a powerful emotion. There are several interlocking and overlapping mechanisms

which produce compulsive, addictive behaviors within one's system.

Biological mechanisms at play involve the dopaminergic pathways triggering one's reward systems, including the limbic system for both initiation of addiction and signaling to the frontal cortex that generates inhibiting control. Volkow theorized in her exploration of the neuroscience of addiction that, "Addiction is a hijacked limbic system" speaking to one's experienced loss of control, as many with experience with substances can attest to (Volkow et al., 2005). The elation experienced when indulging in a substance can be understood within the context of an evolutionary processes that link reward and pleasure-seeking to risk-taking.

Substance use may begin with intense, initial positive experiences, yet becomes uncontrollable when it interacts with human neural chemistry. The human body is built to adapt to survive. The brain exposed to substances learns that they are a viable source of problem solving. Substances become cognitively encoded as a solution to an affective problem by providing powerful affective shift. Resulting decision-making weakens one's ability to turn down the promise of a reward. The research shows that, despite initial positive feelings and emotions, affect does not improve in long run with sustained substance use (Martinez et al., 2004). Negative affect remains the same, as differing experiences of use do not improve one's emotional state. In some cases, negative affect even became worse and more difficult to manage, as emotional regulation strategies became more difficult to use once the body and mind had habituated to low-effort, high-reward situations (Ding et al., 2021).

Over millions of years of evolution, our bodies and brains were built to adapt and give us the best chance of survival. Our bodies can adapt to foreign substances, producing a tolerance, which decreases the subjective and positive feelings the initial dose provided. Increased doses are needed to achieve desired effect, while also our ability to cope with the world around us are depleted. Repeatedly engaging in low effort / high reward stimuli increases the perceived cognitive effort it takes to engage in high effort / medium reward tools, even if they might be better for us in the long run. Understandably, this lowers motivation to pursue alternative forms of coping. One's tolerance for the events of the world around them is lowered while the physical tolerance of the substance is raised. This forms a dependence, and then addiction, in pursuit of previous pleasant feelings or, even just to achieve emotional homeostasis.

Substance use is a form of coping; maladaptive perhaps, but as reasonable as reaching out to any other mechanism people use to get through the difficulties of their lives. What separates substance use and more adaptive coping is the potential for dependency and addiction, leading to lapses in judgement and poor decision-making skills in service of feeding the compulsive habit. Addiction is, at its core, a biological process, with underlying physical mechanisms that interweave to create the platform for chemical dependency. Our bodies respond to rewards, and substances strongly activate the brain reward circuit, leading to intensely positive feelings (MacNicol, 2016). However, those positive feelings come at a cost. Substance use can flood the PFC, the area of the brain in which we conduct executive functions like attention, impulsivity, and inhibition (Bowirrat & Oscar-Berman, 2005). An

8 impacted PFC, focused predominantly on the seeking and satisfying of reward

urges, can lay the groundwork for the cycle of addiction to continue onward.

A prerequisite for addiction is for substances to be introduced to the environment and learned as an available coping strategy. Once that is established, an individual feels a negative affective experience, like depression or anxiety, and reaches out for that substance as a coping tool. The hope is to rectify heightened emotional experiences, or amplify negatively, or absently, felt feeling states. One tries to use substances to feel more joy or feel less pain, but either way to perform some sort of emotional regulatory control in a way the person is otherwise unable to. The cognitive experience and neurological response to the highly stimulating substance then contributes to an individual's sense of personal control, which later in the addiction cycle lapses into a loss of control as other coping and options fail to have the same desired effect. The mesolimbic dopaminergic system has been recognized for its central role in motivated behaviors, various types of reward, and, more recently, in cognitive processes (Alcaro et al., 2007). Within the limbic system, the brain reward circuit and dopaminergic pathways are activated during substance use, creating strong associations between effects of the substance and positive affective states.

However, as previously covered, our bodies are built to adapt. Above all else, that is their primary function. Once a maladaptive coping tool for emotional regulation is used, like substance use, and the reward pathways are activated, the effect on the PFC leads to disinhibition tendencies as well as to increases in physical tolerance levels. More substance is required to reach the same results, leading to increased use and to dependency on substances to establish the same feeling state. This dependency is also a sign that withdrawal could   9 happen, a negative physical and psychological state resulting from being without a substance.

Withdrawal feeds dependency which feeds tolerance. When a person is unable to maintain the same level of intoxication, withdrawal symptoms occur - which can include mood dysregulation like heightened irritability and depression, sleep disturbances, somatic symptoms like sweating, tremor, seizures, and perceptual disturbances like flu-like symptoms, muscle aches, gastric issues (West & Gossop, 1994). In order to avoid these negative symptoms, which range in severity but could even require hospitalization and medical intervention, there is inspiration to continue using, fostering dependency. The more the body adapts to a foreign substance, the higher the levels of tolerance, requiring more of a substance to achieve the same ends. When that amount is unsustainable due to cost or other resources, withdrawal effects can occur, keeping the cycle perpetuating. This, harking back to the learning theory, is a cycle of negative consequences educating one on a future course of action.

When tolerance to a substance becomes high, an individual might use large amounts to achieve the same effect and experience withdrawal symptoms daily. In this case, the aim of continued use is to ameliorate withdrawal symptoms and not just cope with life stressors. The cycle perpetuates a lack of control as one seeks to ameliorate withdrawal but in doing so is increasing their tolerance, needing more of a substance to achieve the same effect. The desire to continuously remain emotionally regulated is appealing to anybody and substances make that level of control possible, while simultaneously the cycle seeks to unseat one's agency as they become trapped in the cycle of avoiding withdrawal symptoms and building tolerance.

The PFC is vital for executive functions, for a wide range of responsibilities including language, spatial learning, conscious thought, judgment, and decision-making (Matlin & Farmer, 2016). This area of the brain is crucial in the regulation of impulsive behaviors by facilitating the inhibition of action and tamping down of impulsivity mechanisms. Typically, the PFC can inhibit pleasure seeking behaviors in favor of other active coping skills and strategies. This part of the brain can assist with assessing consequences, and gauging potential future responses to an action. However, in the case of addiction a 'hijacking' of the PFC occurs, as the dopaminergic pathways underlying the reward drive in the brain are over-engaged, encouraging a superseding of executive decision-making skills (Volkow et al., 2007). With the drive for sensation-seeking activated, as well as diminished activity within the PFC, impulsive thoughts and actions may occur. An underactive PFC combined with an overactive limbic system produces the necessary cerebral environment for decision-making skills to favor short-term solutions such as drugseeking behaviors, and the intensity of the felt pleasure of a reward increases further reinforcement (Volkow et al., 2007).

Neuroadaptation refers to underlying central nervous system changes that occur following repeated use, including the changes that allow a person to develop a tolerance and to experience withdrawal without that substance. Incentive learning mechanisms work hand in hand with neuroadaptation to amplify the reward effect of an activity and punishing effects of abstinence (West & Brown, 2013). Abstinence, leading to felt negatives of withdrawal and increase in anxiety to close the loop and abate the symptoms, is so aversive the inclination towards drug taking is strengthened by these very avoidance learning mechanisms (West & Brown, 2013). The brain is constantly intaking new information and learning ways to adapt to survive. It understands, on a very core level, that a particular substance leads to pleasurable feelings and the desire to maintain that level of pleasure leads to cravings.

Craving is a powerful desire for something, and as such has been seen as a central driving force for ongoing drug use (Weiss et al., 2005). A craving involves several advanced neural biomechanical responses, including altered dopamine activity, disrupted prefrontal control and hyperactive striatal-limbic responses in experiencing drug cues, stress, and drug intake (Sinha, 2013). Alterations in these cortico-limbic-striatal and prefrontal self-control circuits have been used to predict drug craving and relapse risk (Sinha, 2013). Craving can be psychologically felt as a deficit, it is inherently a wanting state, experienced as a negative affective state (Giuliani & Berkman, 2015). When someone stops using, it can lead to a depleted state of desire, resulting in dysphoria and cravings, reinforcing the use of the drug. Cravings put stress on the body and on the brain. This stress can contribute to the disruption of typical function of the PFC. On the basis of fMRI scans, researchers Goldstein and Volkow (2002, 2011) have coined the iRISA model, impaired response inhibition and salience attribution, as the key areas of disrupted typical PFC function in times of craving and addiction. According to their model, this disruption attributes excessive salience to the drug of choice and biological drug-related cues, decreased sensitivity to non-drug reinforcers and decreased ability to inhibit maladaptive or disadvantageous behaviors.

The brain reward circuit is crucial to these processes. There are a few brain neurotransmitters associated with substance use and addiction, the main ones including dopamine, serotonin, norepinephrine and glutamate. These neurotransmitters interact with the dopaminergic pathways, which have crucial functions within the brain. The mesolimbic dopaminergic pathway recognizes reward effects (including recognizing incentives, pleasure, and positive reinforcements), while the mesocortical pathway links the limbic and prefrontal cortical systems and engages the executive functions, which could include decision making and attention paid to differing stimuli (Bowirrat & Oscar-Berman, 2005). The brain reward circuit is a neurobiological mechanism that functions to regulate an individual's response to activities that promote survival. The circuit rewards activities like obtaining food, sex, and social interaction by producing a pleasurable feeling. When intentionally overloaded, the system will produce an intensely pleasurable feeling, which, when paired with other learned behaviors and societal factors, can lead to a desire to reuse the substances that produce that feeling.

The brain reward circuit also triggers hippocampal memory centers to remember the activities, experiences, and environment that led to the reward (Miendlarzewska et al., 2016).
This serves our survival-based biology as a pirate's map to treasure by promoting future similar behavior. These pathways are primarily mediated by dopamine, with increased activity are responsible for the pleasurable feeling associated with rewarding behavior and decreased activity promoting a reengagement in reward-seeking behavior.

Understanding the power of the mesolimbic reward circuit is crucial to understanding the biological and cognitive components of the power of addiction. As one researcher MacNicol (2017) put it,

> The cumulative effect of repeated exposure leads to persistent suppression of the reward circuit to the point that natural rewards can no longer activate it, and the individual exists in a state of discord that can only be interrupted by potent activators of the reward system, such as continued substance use. (p. 142)

A famous animal study explored this by placing electrodes to the brain of rats in order to activate this area of the brain. When activated, rats repeatedly pressed a bar which elicited this response (like a drug), ignoring all other stimuli including food, drink, and mating opportunities, often to the point of starving to death (Olds & Milner, 1954). Even more recent studies have confirmed that high impulsivity can be considered a risk factor for alcohol and drug abuse (Nawi et al., 2021).

Developing a tolerance is a biological process, as a body habituates to the use of a substance it will trigger the reward systems significantly less, requiring larger doses to achieve the same effect. Evolutionarily, this mechanism exists in the body as a benefit to habituate to the world around us. Tolerance exists in many forms, for example a chronically ill patient will develop a high pain tolerance in order to function and survive despite the pain. If substances produce incapacitation, the body tries to adjust so that subjective incapacitation decreases with tolerance. Early PET scans using dopamine have demonstrated decreased mesolimbic dopamine receptor density in chronic substance abusers (Volkow et al., 1993). FMRI scans have further demonstrated that activity is increased during the planning stages of cocaine use but decreased during the period of actual intoxication (Volkow et al., 2019). The response

14 of brain cells is to downregulate receptors and/or decrease the production of

neurotransmitters that are more than normal levels. Pleasurable feelings are decreased from long-term drug use, contrary to the hopes of one desiring to reengage with the initially intense pleasurable feeling.

Impulsivity can also be examined through the lens of either a state or a trait. A state is a temporary place of being, like how anger and sadness are emotional states. In contrast, traits are personality characteristics that are more stable and enduring through the course of time. The neurobiological mechanisms of addiction bolster impulsive states, contributing to higher impulsive decisions and actions during high craving and sensation-seeking states. Trait impulsivity can be a personality risk factor, which can increase through repeated and habitual substance use, contributing to the cycle of craving, use, and withdrawal. After some time and learning, the PFC becomes attuned to those drug cues of cravings and trained towards impaired decision-making. Implementing quick fixes and immediate gains at the expense of long-term and other consequences. Trait impulsivity, therefore, can stand as a risk factor for addictive behaviors and consequences.

The area of the brain that most contributory to executive functioning skills like weighing consequences and decision-making is the PFC. Various substances and the process of addiction contributes to a disinhibited PFC, which can increase impulsivity. Impulsivity is also a character trait that likely involves increased sensitivity to rewards (i.e., sensation seeking) and decreased inhibitory control by these very same mechanisms. The dopaminergic pathway and overactive striatal-limbic responses encourage reward seeking behaviors and diminished activity in the PFC paves the way for impulsive decision-making, producing the necessary bioneural environment for repeated drug use. Various treatments have risen to conquer addiction through the lens of these mechanisms. Physical and psychological courses

of treatment aimed at increasing one's awareness of consequences and correcting

dopaminergic levels to fend off withdrawal to ensure a breaking of the cycle.

Mindfulness can assist other forms of substance use behaviors by addressing

impulsivity mechanisms, circumnavigating cravings and implementing additional

coping for triggers.

Mindfulness

The third wave of cognitive behavioral therapy (CBT) led to the introduction

of mindfulness-based approaches. Mindfulness is most generally defined as

intentionally focusing one's attention in a nonjudgmental way to the experience of

the present moment (Baer et al., 2004). This has significant clinical utility, as clients

are often encouraged to pursue mental health and wellness, framed through

psychological flexibility, or the "ability to be in the present moment with full

awareness and openness to our experience and to take action guided by our values;

or 'be present, open up, and do what matters'" (Harris, 2019).

Many mindfulness practices start with grounding exercises, often attempting

to contact the present moment. One popular tool utilized in mindfulness is

purposeful meditation. During meditation, individuals are often invited to begin

cultivating curiosity, therefore beginning to accept what they are experiencing

without attaching judgements or meaning to passing thoughts and feelings (Shapiro

et al., 2006). Mindfulness can simply be observing what is happening as it is

happening (Anicha et al., 2012). Crucial components of mindfulness include

acknowledging the temporary aspect of sensations, feeling states, and that impulses

are in constant flux (Murphy & MacKillop, 2012). Segal stresses the nonjudgemental element of mindfulness, in which stimuli is evaluated as neither 6

good nor bad, merely present (Segal et al., 2002). This invites a purposeful,

intentional, open awareness and encouraged practitioners to choose how they want to

move forward, rather than acting on impulse (Segal et al., 2002).

Five Facets of Mindfulness

Baer et al. (2006)'s Five Facets of Mindfulness Questionnaire, beyond being an extremely useful tool for research, assists with the codification of an abstract concept like mindfulness. Baer and colleagues conducted a factor analysis of the scores of 613 college students who completed five different mindfulness questionnaires. The analysis generated five separate facets of mindfulness including: observing, describing, acting with awareness, nonjudging of inner experience, and non-reactivity of inner experience (Baer et al., 2006). The observing facet is related to the tendency for individuals to notice external stimuli, such as sights and sounds as well as internal stimuli, such as thoughts and emotions. The describing facet refers to the individual's ability to put their internal experience into words. The acting with awareness facet explains the individual's ability to attend to the activities they are undertaking in the present moment. The non-judging of inner experience facet is related to assessing one's internal experiences as neither good nor bad. And finally, the non-reactivity to inner experience facet is related to the individual's ability to simply notice one's thoughts and feelings without acting on them (Baer et al., 2006).

Mechanisms of Mindfulness

The root of mindfulness is intentionality. Ideally, purposeful control inhibits compulsivity in neural mechanisms, so when the prefrontal cortex is activated, the limbic system response can be intentionally inhibited. By amplifying the frontal cortical system, the reward drive is lowered, allowing for the decrease in impulsivity to sate sensation-seeking, reward-driven behaviors. This might be achieved through the five facets, allowing for trait impulsivity to be decreased through greater inhibitory control. Linking to Volkow's description of a 'hijacked limbic system', mindfulness directly taps into the cognitive control system, boosting inhibitory techniques and attentional control to inhibit substance use or other maladaptive behaviors.

Another way of describing 'intentionality' is the mindful, purposeful, direction of attention. Within the brain mechanisms, the anterior cingulate cortex directs the spotlight of attention. The PFC needs to be activated in order to inhibit the mesocortical pathway so attention can be refined and focused on specific stimuli. Studies have demonstrated through fMRI findings that following an eight-week mindfulness-based cognitive therapy course, patients with bipolar disorder showed significant improvements in mindfulness, emotion regulation, and reduced anxiety, which was attributed to activations in the medial PFC (Ives-Deliperi et al., 2013).

Studies have shown that people with experience in meditation [utilizing a tool with which to practice mindful awareness and attentional control] present with overall increased connectivity within attentional networks, as well as between attentional regions and medial frontal cortical regions (Hasenkamp & Barsalou, 2012). Studies dove into these brain mechanisms even further, postulating that with the regular practice of mindfulness, attention is directed toward the limbic pathway for present-moment sensory awareness; these regions involve the thalamus, insula, and primary sensory regions (Farb et al., 2012). Malinowski has written extensively on the central

18   role that attentional control mechanisms play in the development and utilization of

mindfulness skills. They found, "attentional resources are allocated more fully during early processing phases which subsequently enhance further processing" (Malinowski et al., 2013, p. 1). Attentional resources allocated early on when mindfully attending to surroundings through focus instead of a periphery process increases intentional control, yielding benefits of mindfulness like increased attention span, concentration, and focus (Kabat-Zinn, 2003).

Further studies hypothesize a crux of mindfulness lies in its disidentification ability, which elicits the dampening of emotional responsivity, and separates oneself from the triggering stimulus through the processes of nonreactivity. Bernstein et al.'s research dove into selfdistanced perspective, cognitive distancing, and cognitive defusion as key tools for mental health treatment (2015). Hede (2017) furthered the concept of cognitive defusion, defined here as

"enabling people to disconnect from their own dysfunctional thoughts." Defusion is a skill that is aimed at detaching one from one's thoughts, emotions and judgements, both future, past and present. Viewing thoughts as passing words/sensations, one can let them go, be present, and focus on the broader experience, as opposed to becoming stuck in one absolute truth.

A potential complementary mechanism on how mindfulness can assist with attentional control and decrease impulsivity in drinking lies in the action identification theory (Vallacher & Wegner, 1987). This theory proposes that actions exist within various levels of abstraction. For example, drinking requires both perceived low-level action of swallowing a liquid because it exists purely neutral physical sensation without judgement, and a high-level abstraction of experiencing

19 joy, a non-neutral emotional experience. Defusion and disidentification go hand in

hand with this theory, as this concept attempts to de-identify and defamiliarize an

action to the actor, thereby enabling detachment and defusion techniques to become

easier to implement. By defamiliarizing oneself with an action identity, it becomes

less triggering to maneuver around. Mindfulness, with its disidentification properties

and present-moment focus, can aid individuals in the ability to shift meaning behind

action from a high-level representation to a low-level representation. One study

assessed 125 undergraduate psychology students, results "supporting the hypothesis

that high-level action identification partially mediates the relation between

mindfulness and dyscontrolled drinking" (Schellas et al., 2016, p. 51). Mindfulness

can be key in removing thoughts and actions associated with triggers and cravings,

lowering impulsivity encouraged by biomechanisms. This brings much to light about

how mindfulness may improve self-restraint and overall control mechanisms through

altering the way we interpret situations.

Interactions Between Alcohol Use, Impulsivity and Mindfulness

Research has demonstrated that impulsivity is a risk factor for alcohol misuse and

that mindfulness can assist with the reduction of impulsivity. One study explored

relations among urgency, mindfulness, and substance use in adolescence by

collecting data from students ($N = 1,051$) at a large private high school in the Pacific

Northwest (Robinson et al., 2014). They found urgency was a key factor in indicating

higher substance use, and mindfulness was explored as a mediator, yielding a lower

likelihood of marijuana and alcohol use over the course of the lifetime. A similar

study explored if mindfulness skills moderate the relation between negative urgency

and drinking to cope, targeting college student drinkers instead of adolescents.

Interestingly, they found the mindfulness skill of accepting without judgment

20   significantly dampened the positive relation between negative urgency and drinking

to cope (Hoyer & Correia, 2020). Further assessing college students, another study

examined the moderating role of mindfulness (measured through mindfulness versus

a relaxed group and control group) on impulsivity and negative affect, positive affect,

and urge to drink among college students with atrisk drinking habits (Vinci et al.,

2016). Analyses showed that the relationship between trait impulsivity and affective

state and urge to drink significantly differed for participants who underwent

mindfulness versus relaxation interventions. Participants were given one of three

interventions: mindfulness, relaxation, or control, and given several self-report

measures before and after the interventions to assess their negative affect, positive

affect, and urge to drink. Of their many findings, primary to this study, the

mindfulness intervention yielded a positive association between negative urgency

and the urge to drink. For those who received the mindfulness intervention, higher

levels of some facets of trait impulsivity (Sensation Seeking, Negative Urgency, and

Positive Urgency) were associated with higher levels of negative affect and urge and

lower levels of positive affect. They found that the impulsivity subscale was crucial

in evaluating the mindfulness intervention's effectivity, as positive associations were

found between the impulsivity subscales of Sensation Seeking and Negative Urgency

and state mindfulness. They also found that decreases in the impulsivity facet of (lack

of) Perseverance after the mindfulness intervention were associated with increased

Positive Affect.

Gallo et al. (2021) investigated the relationship between different facets of

mindfulness and impulsivity among people with alcohol use disorder (AUD) with

adults in an inpatient setting in Brazil. They administered the self-report measures:

the Alcohol Use Disorders

21   Identification Test (AUDIT), the Five Facets of Mindfulness Questionnaire (FFMQ-

SF), and the Short UPPS-P Impulsive Behavior Scale (SUPPS-P), to 165

participants. Their studies suggested that higher mindfulness skills were related to

lower reported impulsive traits. One study found mindfulness-based treatments to be

significant in 6-month smoking cessation compared to a control group, which used a

tobacco quit line and nicotine patches (Davis et al., 2014). Compared to controls,

the mindfulness treatment group reported a successful 6-month abstinence,

confirmed by carbon monoxide breath testing and a follow-up measure.

Some studies explored craving as the impetus between impulsivity and alcohol

treatment relapse. One study postulated that craving is a mediating factor between

Impulsive Personality Traits (IPT) and relapse during AUD treatment (Reichl et al.,

2022). They assessed an inpatient population with a primary AUD diagnosis ($N =$

320) and found that attentional as well as nonplanning IPT's were associated with

higher levels of craving. This research was extended when exploring the multiple

facets of craving as well as emotion regulatory experiences (Cheng et al., 2022). This

team found that increased levels of stress were associated with increased craving

intensity, imagery, and intrusiveness. High levels of anxiety and high levels of

craving imagery were also positively associated. In times of duress, increased

impulsivity and heightened craving experiences make emotional regulation

significantly more difficult, which could make treatment goals and abstinence more

difficult as well.

Cavicchioli et al. (2019) attempted to uncover the mediating role of

mindfulness between difficulty with emotion regulation and AUD. They used the

domains of mindfulness selfregulation of attention and acceptance-based ideas,

22   subscales assessed through the Mindful Attention Awareness Scale, MAAS) and Five

Facet Mindfulness Questionnaire, FFMQ. They found mindfulness to be a protective factor for difficulty with emotion regulation effects for individuals with AUD. It was found that cravings can produce negative emotional states, which could make mindfulness practice even more impactful and useful. As for emotional regulation, one study explored the unique niche of higher education faculty and the covid pandemic with emotional difficulties, impulsivity and mindfulness (Weyandt et al., 2020). They found lower mindfulness levels and greater measured impulsivity were associated with higher rates of anxiety and depression.

The role of past negative, even traumatic, experiences cannot be dismissed when discussing substance use. One study explored how mindfulness can mediate early experiences of adversity and current alcohol use and consequences, by assessing undergraduate students ($N = 385$) at a midwestern university (Brett et al., 2018). They discovered that higher levels of adversity and lower levels of mindfulness predicted alcohol experiences and alcohol-related consequences. They also hypothesized based on their findings that mindfulness might mediate the relationship between early adversity and alcohol outcomes.

In summary, neural chemistry, when impacted by addiction, inhibits the PFC and overengages the striatal-limbic and dopaminergic pathways. This dampens the body's decisionmaking processes, which then lose sight of negative long-term consequences and introduces misperception of risk, and consequently prioritizes immediate relief of negative sensations and quick rewards. This is directly seen in the impulsivity mechanisms, central to the worsening of drinking-related consequences. Research has demonstrated that impulsivity is a risk factor for

23 alcohol misuse, especially when it comes to reaction to craving imagery and to

negative emotional states. Mindfulness, with its features of defusion and present-moment focus, can aide with drinking harm reduction through the peripheral reduction of impulsivity.

Chapter III: Methodology

This study's procedures were approved by the Adler IRB, protocol #23-023.

Description of Study Design

This study utilized a between-participants design and utilized correlation and regression statistical analyses. This study obtained a participant's self-reported impulsivity score using the UPPS-P (urgency, premeditation, perseverance, sensation seeking, and positive urgency), their factors of mindfulness scores using the Five Facet Mindfulness Questionnaire, as well as explored the scope of drinking behaviors with a quantity and frequency questionnaire as well as the Drinker Inventory of Consequences. The research conducted sought to replicate previous research on correlations between facets of impulsivity and mindfulness and to test the mediating role of mindfulness on association between facets of impulsivity and drinking-related problems.

Description of the Population

Researchers conducted an a priori power analysis to compute the required sample size necessary to give this study enough power to correctly reject the null hypothesis. GPower version 3.1.9 application (Faul et al., 2009) was used to calculate a priori power with the following parameters: Alpha was set at .05, power at 80%, and effect size specified to be small-medium. Power analysis produced a desired sample size of 124. After filtering out respondents who did not fully complete the battery or otherwise had unorthodox answers (such as only answering "d" across all questions for all questionnaires), the final N was 146 participants. Validity checks were utilized, including asking a bogus question between measures ("please select option B to continue").

Previous research has been conducted largely amongst young adult and/or in-patient populations. This study extended previous literature by examining adult participants from the general population. Age was assessed via a self-report question, included within the demographics questionnaire, which presented participants with a categorical classification to self-select. Age ranges were between 18 and 55. The most common category of age identification endorsed was 30 – 35 years old, with 52% of the total participants endorsing this age range (n = 76). The second highest category of age identification was 24 – 29 years old participants, with 25% of the total participants endorsing (n = 37). This means 80% of the sample was 35 years old or younger, yet only 4 respondents were 18 – 23 years of age. Education was also assessed in the demographic's questionnaire, with the highest category being 69% (n = 100) who completed a Bachelor's degree or less, with 9% (n = 13) completing some master's level coursework. Ethnicity: 95% (n = 139) of the population sample endorsed identifying as White or Caucasian, with 4% (n = 5) identifying as Black or African American. The majority identified as a cisgender woman, 37% (n = 54), or a cisgender man (33%, n = 49), but there were 19% (n = 28) who identify as a transgender man, and 8% (n = 12) of respondents who identify as a transgender woman. Sexual orientation included 53% of the sample identified as heterosexual (n = 78), with 33% (n = 48) as bisexual and 8% (n = 12) as asexual. Economically, 63.7% said that they are at $59,000 or lower for an annual household income, with the highest indcividual category being $50 - 59,000 at 17% of the sample. Participants also responded to the question,

26   "How important would you say religion is in your life?" with 40% (*n* = 56) selecting

"very important" and 28% (*n* = 41) selecting "moderately important." Only 1.4% (*n*

= 2) selected the

"not at all" choice. Responding to "What is your current religious identity?" a

majority of the sample, 80% (*n* = 116), identified themselves as Christian.

Recruitment Procedures

Participants were recruited through the online recruitment method Amazon Mechanical

Turk (MTurk), and they were compensated $0.50 for completing the study. MTurk

is a tool which helps businesses and/or researchers create "tasks" for things like

personal experience and opinion surveys, and MTurk facilitates compensation for

the "workers" who have completed them.

Consent Procedures

Informed consent was obtained as part of the survey procedure process,

highlighting that study procedures are anonymous and pose minimal risks.

Participants were provided with information about the proposed study prior to being

exposed to assessment materials, and participants had the opportunity to self-select

and provide their consent or choose not to participate in the study. Efforts to ensure

anonymity of data were taken, such as using the platform Qualtrics to protect

participant data and not recording participant names or other identifying

information. All data from this study was aggregated into cumulative results to

further ensure anonymity.

Measures

Demographics Questionnaire.

 Participants were asked to complete a demographics questionnaire with their

age, highest year of completed education, ethnicity, country of residency, gender

identity, sexual orientation, annual household income, religious identity and prior

meditation experience (see Appendix A). Specifications like country of origin were

included due to the online nature of recruitment measures; MTurk is an Internet

marketplace, where international participants can become "workers" and complete

surveys. Meditation experience was elicited as one way to determine how much

experience participants had with a primary tool of mindfulness and rehearsal they

have had with mindfulness skills. Within the demographics questionnaire, an

operational definition on meditation was included and prior experience was elicited.

The specific verbiage included: "For the purposes of this study, "meditation" is

defined as concentrated effort to focus one's mind. This can involve muscle

relaxation, specific techniques, and/or heightened awareness. With that definition in

mind, how much prior experience do you have with meditation?". 35% of

participants ($n = 52$, a majority) said "regular practice, weekly" (*see table

4).* A "drink" was also operationally defined as, "For the purposes of this study, a

standard drink is considered 14 grams of alcohol, found in 12 oz of beer, 5 oz of

wine, and/or 1.5 oz of distilled spirits" (see Appendix A). With this in mind,

quantity, frequency, binging and general drinking habits of the sample were also

collected. Quantity was assessed, "During the past 12 months, how many alcoholic

drinks did you have on a typical day when you drank alcohol?" with the largest

numerical category being "16 – 18" ($n = 26$, 17.8%). Frequency was assessed,

"During the past 12 months, how often did you usually have any kind of drink

containing alcohol?" with the largest category being "2 times a week" ($n = 28$,

19.2%). Binge drinking habits were assessed, "During the past 12 months,   28 how

often do you have 5 or more drinks on one occasion?" with the largest category

being "monthly" (*n = 50,* 34.2%). Max drinking was assessed "During the past 12

months, what is the largest number of drinks containing alcohol that you drank

within a 24-hour period?" with the largest numerical category being "8 – 11" (*n =*

29,

19.9%; see Table 2).

UPPS-P

The *UPPS-P* is a self-report measure comprising of 59 items, with 10-14

items per scale (Whiteside & Lynam, 2001). Items are scored on a 4-point scale

(agree strongly, agree some, disagree some, disagree strongly), with higher values

translating into higher levels of impulsivity. The *UPPS-P* was created by Whiteman

& Lynam to further fetter out the multiple facets behind impulsive behaviors. The

facets are rooted in the Five Factor Model of personality (McCrae & Costa, 1990),

and Whiteside & Lynam utilized the NEO-PI-R and other impulsivity measures

(EASI-III Impulsivity Scales [Buss & Plomin, 1975], Dickman's Functional and

Dysfunctional Impulsivity Scales [Dickman, 1990], Barratt Impulsiveness Scale –

11 [BIS-11;

Patton et al, 1995], I-7 Impulsiveness Questionnaire [I-7; Eysenck, Pearson, Easting & Allsopp,

1985], Personality Research Form Impulsivity Scale [PRF; Jackson, 1984], Multidimensional

Personality Questionnaire Control Scale [MPQ; Tellegen, 1982], Temperament and

Character Inventory [TCI; Cloninger et al., 1991], Sensation Seeking Scale [SSS;

Zuckerman, 1994]). The research team administered these scales to 437 college-aged students, and then analyzed their results through exploratory factor analysis. This analysis identified four distinct personality facets (internal consistencies in parentheses): urgency (0.87), deliberation (0.91), persistence (0.82), and sensation seeking (0.90), (Cyders, 2007). In this study's sample, the alpha's were: negative urgency (0.72), lack of premeditation (0.89), lack of perseverance (0.59), sensation seeking (0.91), and positive urgency (0.91).

Five Facets of Mindfulness

The Five Facet Mindfulness Questionnaire (FFMQ; Baer et al, 2006) is a widely used self-report measure aimed to assess mindfulness tendencies in daily life. Items were developed by integrating from the Mindful Attention Awareness Scale (MAAS; Brown & Ryan, 2003), Freiburg Mindfulness Inventory (FMI; Buchheld et al., 2001), Kentucky Inventory of

Mindfulness Skills (KIMS; Baer et al., 2004), Cognitive and Affective Mindfulness Scale (CAMS; Feldman et al., 2007), and the Mindfulness Questionnaire (MQ; Chadwick et al., 2005).

The 39-item measure is designed to assess mindfulness across five factors (coefficient alphas):

Observing (.84), Describing (.87), Acting with Awareness (.87), Nonreactivity (.75), and Nonjudging (.88) (Fernandez, 2010). Participants are asked to rate how true statements are for themselves on a five-point Likert-type scale (1 *rarely true* to 5 *very often or always true*). A scree plot suggested the five-factor model with a hierarchical structure. In this study's sample, the alpha's were: observing (0.84), describing (0.23 – did not utilize this construct due to the low alpha), acting with awareness (0.84), nonreactivity (0.81), nonjudging (0.80). The describing construct was not utilized considering the low alpha.

Alcohol consumption was assessed using a standard format relating to quantity and frequency of drinking over the last 12 months. Questions reinforced that the time period respondents should reflect on were their most recent drinking habits, as opposed to lifelong trends (see Appendix B).

Drinker Inventory of Consequences

The Drinker Inventory of Consequences (DrInC; Miller et al., 1995) is a 45-item overall measure of alcohol-related consequences, with higher scores reflecting greater consequence severity. The original study assessed 1382 participants from 11 participating sites. A more recent study (Forcehimes et al., 2007) examined the psychometrics and found the DrInC to be reliable, valid, and clinically useful, with the DrInC subscales to be internally consistent and nonredundant. Forcehimes et al. explored the five consequence subscales (coefficient alphas): Physical Consequences (.72), Interpersonal Consequences (.87), Intrapersonal Consequences (.87), Impulse Control (.77), and Social Responsibility (.81), demonstrating that the subscales possess sufficient intercorrelation strength and item breadth. However, according to Forcehimes et al., the normed chi-square (8.7), goodness-of-fit (.73), confirmatory fit index (.71), and the root mean squared error of approximation (.08) for the DrInC all suggested a poor to modest statistical fit to the facevalid 5 factor model. Consequently, in a recent study, researchers Kirouac and

Witkiewitz (2018) explored the DrInC's psychometric properties, and their results indicated the five subscales had poor construct validity and were noninvariant across time. They suggested the use of a newly developed three-factor model, consisting of mild, moderate, and severe consequences. Kirouac and Witkiewitz found these had "excellent" psychometric properties, including good internal consistency reliability, construct validity, and measurement invariance over time. This study examined the bivariate correlation of the individual facets, and then determined, as per recommendations from previous research, utilizing the total score for hypothesis testing would be best practices.

Chapter IV: Results Descriptive Statistics

After excluding incomplete and invalid measures, 146 participants completed the surveys in full. Table 5 provides descriptive statistics, including means and standard deviations for all variables.

Correlations

Mediators are variables that contribute to an indirect relationship by linking two variables to suggest an effect on the process of the relationship. These variables can contribute to a deeper understanding of why and how a cause leads to an outcome, and they are conceptualized as the mechanism through which the independent variable influences the dependent variable (Baron & Kenny, 1986). Figure 1 is a simple mediation model illustrating this relationship in the present study. Impulsivity, measured through the UPPS, acted as the quasi-independent variable. Drinking-related consequences, as measured through the DrInC, acted as the dependent variable. Mindfulness, as measured through the FFMQ, is the mediating variable M. The pathways between these variables were labeled a, b, and c and represented direct pathways. The direct pathways needed to demonstrate statistically significant effects in bivariate correlations for mediation to be tested. Mediation is tested by estimating an indirect pathway, which combines the direct pathways a and b.

Bivariate correlations testing the direct pathways were analyzed in Statistical Package for the Social Sciences (SPSS), Version 29.0.2.0. Pathway a (UPPS to FFMQ) had ten correlations with statistical significance (*see Table 6*). These were in the expected direction, indicating that greater trait impulsivity was correlated with lower mindfulness. In Pathway b (FFMQ to DrInC), there were ten correlations in the expected direction with statistical significance, indicating that higher levels of some facets of mindfulness were correlated with lower levels of drinking-related consequences. Specifically, the Acting with Awareness and Nonjudging subscales were in the expected direction, whereas the Observing and Nonreactivity subscales were not in the expected direction (see Table 7). In Pathway c (DrInC to UPPS), the correlations between Lack of Premeditation and Lack of Perseverance were correlated in the expected direction with statistical significance, indicating those domains of impulsivity yielded higher risky drinking behaviors. Negative Urgency, Sensation Seeking and Positive Urgency were correlated in an unexpected direction with all DrInC subscales, yet those domains also did not demonstrate statistical significance (see Table 8).

Hypothesis Testing

Having confirmed that many of the variables examined in this study were indeed correlated significantly as part of first hypothesis test, the mediation analysis was utilized to test the second hypothesis. Drinking-related consequences were seen to be the most unified construct with all subscales showing associations with other variables in the expected direction and with comparable effect sizes, so the total score of the DrInC was utilized for subsequent mediation analyses. Impulsivity and mindfulness correlations varied among the subscales, with some subscales correlating with other variables in a direction opposite to the original prediction. Correlation coefficients that were opposite of expected direction were not included in 34 mediation analyses. Based on the pattern of correlations, eight mediation analyses were run. The variables included: a single DrInC Total Score (n = 146, M = 111.4, SD = 24.1); two subscales of the UPPS including Lack of Premeditation (n = 146, M = 23.1, SD = 6.3), and Lack of Perseverance (n = 146, M = 21.9, SD = 4.0); and four subscales of the FFMQ including Observing (n = 146, M =

26.7, SD = 5.8), Nonreactivity (n = 146, M = 24.3, SD = 4.8), Acting with Awareness (n = 146, M = 22.2, SD = 6.3), and Nonjudging (n = 146, M = 23.9, SD = 5.4).

The UPPS subscales (Positive and Negative Urgency and Sensation-Seeking) that were not included in mediation analyses had non-significant associations or correlations in an unexpected direction with the DrInC total score, and so their path c was not adequate to test mediation. FFMQ Describing subscale was not included in mediation analysis due to a low Cronbach's alpha.

Following A. F. Hayes' (2013) Process macro for SPSS simple mediation model (model 4) was used to test the mediational effect when the indirect effect (IE) of impulsivity on drinking-related consequence via mindfulness (IE = path a x path b; a = the association of impulsivity with the mediator of mindfulness, b = the association between mindfulness and drinking-related consequences). The bias in estimation of 95% CI around the

IE was corrected by modeling 5000 bootstrap re-samples. We accepted the IE as statistically significant only if its bias corrected 95% CI excluded zero.

Observing Mediating Relationship Between Lack of Premeditation and Drinking

Eight mediational analyses were run in SPSS. The first analysis utilized drinkingrelated consequences (measured with the DrInC total score) as the dependent variable, impulsivity (measured with the UPPS subscale, Lack of Premeditation) as the quasiindependent variable, and mindfulness (measured with the FFMQ subscale, Observe) as the mediator variable. The regression model containing direct effects (paths a & b) as well as the IE was statistically significant ($F(2, 143) = 24.84$, $p < .001$) and R^2 was .26. The results showed that path c (i.e., Lack of Premeditation direct effect on DrInC) was not statistically significant (B = .40, $t = 1.39$, $p = .17$) and path b (i.e., direct effect of Observe on DrInC Total Score) was statistically significant (B = 1.95, $p < .001$). Finally, when mindfulness facet Observe was estimated as the IE, the regression coefficient B was .52 and CI(.21, .84) did not include zero and was statistically significant. This means the Observe mindfulness facet acted as a full mediator for the relationship between impulsivity and drinking. Hence, Observe was considered a full mediator for Lack of Premeditation on drinking-related consequences.

Acting with Awareness Mediating Relationship Between Lack of Premeditation and

Drinking Consequences

The second analysis utilized drinking-related consequences (measured with the DrInC total score) as the Y variable, impulsivity (measured with the UPPS subscale, Lack of Premeditation) as the X variable, and mindfulness (measured with the FFMQ subscale, Acting with Awareness) as the M variable. The regression model containing direct effects (paths a & b) as well

as the IE was statistically significant ($F(2, 143) = 32.21$, $p < .001$) and R^2 was

.31. The results showed that path c (i.e., Lack of Premeditation association

with DrInC) B = .23, $t = .82$, $p = .42$ was not statistically significant and path

b (i.e., Acting with Awareness association with DrInC Total Score) B = -2.05,

$p = <.001$ was significant. Finally, when mindfulness facet Acting with

Awareness was estimated as IE (B = .69), the 95% Confidence Interval = .29

to 1.07 did not include zero. Hence, Acting with Awareness was considered a

full mediator for Lack of Premeditation on Drinking-related Consequences.

Nonreactivity Mediating Relationship Between Lack of Premeditation and Drinking

Consequences

The third analysis utilized drinking-related consequences (measured with the

DrInC total score) as the Y variable, impulsivity (measured with the UPPS subscale,
Lack of Premeditation) as the X variable and mindfulness (measured with the

FFMQ subscale, Nonreactivity) as the M variable. The regression model

containing direct effects (paths a & b) as well as the IE was statistically

significant ($F(2, 143) = 23.43$, $p < .001$) and R^2 was .25. The results showed

nonsignificant path c (i.e., Lack of Premeditation association with DrInC), (B

= .41, $t = 1.42$, $p = .15$) and significant path b (i.e., Nonreactivity on Total

Score) B = 2.3, $t = 5.97$, $p < .001$). Finally, when mindfulness facet

Nonreactivity was estimated as IE (B = .51, CI[.19,82]), there was statistical

insignificance, indicating full mediation by Nonreactivity of the association

between Lack of Premeditation on Drinking-related Consequences.

Nonjudging Mediating Relationship Between Lack of Premeditation and Drinking

The fourth analysis utilized drinking-related consequences (measured with the

DrInC total score) as the Y variable, impulsivity (measured with the UPPS subscale,

Lack of

Premeditation) as the X variable, and mindfulness (measured with the FFMQ

subscale, Nonjudging) as the M variable. The regression model containing direct

effects (paths a & b) as well as the IE was statistically significant ($F(2, 143) =$

29.74, $p < .001$) and R^2 was .30. The results showed a non-significant path c (i.e.,

Lack of Premeditation association with DrInC) (B = .19, $t = 66$, $p > .05$) and

significant path b (i.e., Nonjudging association with DrInC Total Score),

(B = -2.32, $t = -6.90$, $p < .001$). Finally, when mindfulness facet Nonjudging was
estimated as

IE, B = .73, CI (.323, 1.126), there statistical insignificance, indicating full mediation.

Hence, Nonjudging is considered a full mediator for Lack of Premeditation on

Drinking-related

Consequences.
Observing Mediating Relationship Between Lack of Perseverance and Drinking

Consequences

The fifth analysis utilized drinking-related consequences (measured with the

DrInC total score) as the Y variable, impulsivity (measured with the UPPS

subscale, Lack of Perseverance) as the X variable and the FFMQ Observing

subscale as the M variable. The regression model containing direct effects

(paths a & b) as well as the IE was statistically significant ($F(2, 143) = 26.82$,

$p < .001$) and R^2 was .27. The results showed that path c (i.e., Lack of

Perseverance association with DrInC) B = .99, $t = 2.22$, $p < .05$) and path b (i.e.,

Observing association with DrInC Total Score), (B = 1.9, t = 6.1, p < .001) 38

were both statistically significant. Finally, when mindfulness facet Observing

was estimated as IE, the regression coefficient B = .72, had 95% CI (.21, 1.25),

indicating statistical insignificance. The significant IE in presence of

significant direct effect of X on Y (path c) suggests that variance in drinking

problems was accounted by both, IE through M and by X. Hence, Observing

is considered a partial mediator for Lack of Perseverance on Drinking-related

Consequences.

Acting with Awareness Mediating Relationship Between Lack of Perseverance and

Drinking Consequences

The sixth analysis utilized drinking-related consequences (measured with the

DrInC total score) as the Y variable, impulsivity (measured with the UPPS

subscale, Lack of Perseverance) as the X variable and mindfulness

(measured with the FFMQ subscale, Acting with Awareness) as the M

variable. The regression model containing direct effects (paths a & b) as

well as the IE was statistically significant ($F(2, 143)$ =

33.74, p < .001) and R^2 was .32. The results showed a non-significant path c (i.e., Lack of

Perseverance association with DrInC) B = .73, t = 1.67, p >.05, and significant path

b (i.e., Acting with Awareness on Total Score) B = -1.99, t = -7.1, p < .001. Finally,

when mindfulness facet Acting with Awareness was estimated as IE, B = .98,

CI(.38, 1.57), there was statistical insignificance, indicating full mediation. Hence,

Acting with Awareness is considered a full mediator for Lack of Perseverance on

Drinking-related Consequences.

 Nonjudging Mediating Relationship Between Lack of Perseverance and Drinking

Consequences

The seventh analysis utilized drinking-related consequences (measured with the

DrInC total score) as the Y variable, impulsivity (measured with the UPPS

subscale, Lack of Perseverance) as the X variable, and mindfulness

(measured with the FFMQ subscale, Nonjudging) as the M variable. The

regression model containing direct effects (paths a & b) as well as the IE was

statistically significant ($F(2, 143) = 31.26$, $p < .001$) and R^2 was .30. The

results showed the path c (i.e., Lack of Perseverance association with DrInC)

B = .71, $t = 1.61$, $p = .11$ was not significant and path b (i.e., Nonjudging

association with Total Score) B = -2.22, $t = -6.78$, $p < .001$ was significant.

Finally, when mindfulness facet Nonjudging was estimated as IE, B = .99,

CI(.36, 1.59), there was statistical insignificance, indicating full mediation.

Hence, Nonjudging is considered a full mediator for Lack of Perseverance on

Drinking-related Consequences.

Nonreactivity Mediating Relationship Between Lack of Perseverance and Drinking

Consequences

The eighth analysis utilized drinking-related consequences (measured

with the DrInC total score) as the Y variable, impulsivity (measured with the

UPPS subscale, Lack of Perseverance) as the X variable and mindfulness

(measured with the FFMQ subscale, Nonreactivity) as the M variable. The

regression model containing direct effects (paths a & b) as well as the IE was statistically significant ($F(2, 143) = 25.14$, $p < .001$) and R^2 was .26. The results

showed the path c (i.e., Lack of Perseverance association with

DrInC) B = .97, $t = 2.15$, $p = .03$ was statistically significant and path b (i.e.,

Nonreactivity association with Total Score) B = 2.23, $t = 5.89$, $p < .001$ was

also statistically significant. Finally, when mindfulness facet of Nonreactivity

was estimated as IE, B = .74, CI(.21, 1.26), there was statistical

insignificance, indicating partial mediation. Hence, Nonreactivity is

considered as a partial mediator for Lack of

Perseverance on Drinking-related Consequences.

Chapter V: Discussion

This study assessed specific facets within trait mindfulness which could be used to mediate the risk between trait impulsivity and drinking-related consequences. Traits are personality characteristics that are more stable, and typically endure through the course of time. Prior research demonstrates that trait impulsivity can be a risk factor for drinking-related behaviors and consequences (Gallo et al., 2021; Peters et al., 2011; Robinson et al., 2014). Murphy and MacKillop (2012) also discovered that problematic alcohol use was positively associated with facets of impulsivity. The current study replicated this finding as two impulsivity subscales (Lack of Premeditation and Lack of Perseverance) were cross-sectionally directly related to drinking-related problems.

Prior research has also explored the connections between mindfulness, trait impulsivity, and drinking-related behaviors (Murphy & MacKillop, 2012; Vinci et al., 2016). Robinson et al. (2014) explored mindfulness as a mediator, and their study found adolescent participants who endorsed higher levels of mindful awareness yielded a lower likelihood of marijuana and alcohol use over the course of the lifetime. More recently, Royuela-Colomer et al. (2021) also found a negative association between mindfulness and impulsivity. Gallo et al. (2021) as well, found that

"higher mindfulness skills were related to lower reported impulsive traits". They found specifically that the domains most strongly related to alcohol dependence were negative urgency and lack of premeditation.

The research as such is robust in utilizing specific facets when identifying an association between trait impulsivity and risky behaviors regarding alcohol, and

42   utilizing mindfulness as a potential mediator. Vinci et al. (2016) utilized a college-

aged participant pool to explore many specific facets of mindfulness as a mediator for trait impulsivity and urge to drink. Their study found that the impulsivity subscale was crucial in evaluating the mindfulness intervention's effectivity; positive associations were found between the impulsivity subscales of Sensation Seeking and Negative Urgency, and state mindfulness. They also found that decreases in the impulsivity facet of (lack of) Perseverance after the mindfulness intervention were associated with increased Positive Affect. The authors here specifically postulate that "mindfulness and impulsivity … are distinct constructs when examined individually (i.e., variation exists regarding which facets of mindfulness versus facets of impulsivity are associated alcohol use behaviors)," (p.367) an argument supported by researchers Murphy and MacKillop (2012). This indicates that mindfulness and impulsivity are not unified constructs and interact with variables in unique ways.

This study found that impulsivity and mindfulness correlations, as well as correlations of both with drinking-related behavior, varied along the unique subscales and facets, with some correlating in a direction opposite to the original prediction. The Observing and Nonreactivity facets of mindfulness were directly correlated with higher drinking-related consequences, which was unexpected. One possible explanation is that people who are observing and non-reacting are not engaging in active responses with issues as they arise. They may be more likely to observe and accept problems vs launching into action in response to stimuli. They also are not disassociating or avoiding and would therefore be more likely to be able to name the consequences they have experienced from drinking. Positive Urgency, Negative Urgency and Sensation Seeking were also correlated in an unexpected direction, with

43   high impulsivity facet scores yet lower drinking-related consequence scores. These

connections are supported by some of the past literature In Vinci et al.'s (2016) study those who demonstrated high Positive Urgency, Negative Urgency, and Sensation Seeking were associated with higher levels of negative affect and urge. They were also susceptible to increased binge-drinking behaviors. One explanation for these associations, but lower drinking-related consequences, might be that those with higher impulsive traits on these scales are more likely to drink too heavily all at once, but once a more positive affect is developed, they might be more inclined to stop before reaching more serious consequences. Vinci et al. also found that decreases in the impulsivity facet of (lack of) Perseverance after the mindfulness intervention were associated with increased Positive

Affect.

Summary of Findings

As such, for this study mediation analyses included the DrInC total score, two subscales of the UPPS that had significant positive correlations with DrInC, including Lack of

Premeditation and Lack of Perseverance, and four subscales of the FFMQ, including Observing,

Nonreactivity, Acting with Awareness, and Nonjudging. Prior research (Kirouac & Witkiewitz, 2018) recommended utilizing the DrInC total score or a three-factor model consisting of mild, moderate, and severe consequences. Literature also found the "Describing" facet of the FFMQ to inconsistently predict alcohol-related behaviors or be otherwise not associated with alcoholrelated cravings (Hoyer & Correia, 2020; Murphy & MacKillop, 2012; Reynolds et al., 2015); the facet also did not have sufficient reliability as estimated with Cronbach's alpha.

Mediational Model 1 (Observing as the variable mediating the relationship between Lack of Premeditation and Drinking Consequences) indicated that Observing acted as a full mediator for the relationship between impulsivity and drinking. Lack of Premeditation assesses acting without considering potential consequences. Cavicchioli et al. (2023) stated that "a core impulsive personality domain across different SUDs includes the tendency to act without thinking or considering the long-term consequences of one's own behaviors (i.e., lack of premeditation)". Coskunpinar et al. (2013) also found "lack of premeditation" domain to be associated with AUDs. Cavicchioli (2019) examined self-regulation of attention as a domain of mindfulness, and found it to be a protective factor for individuals with alcohol use disorder.

Researchers Murphy and MacKillop (2012) found "to be experientially aware of experiences was inversely associated with alcohol involvement." Observing entails utilizing sensory awareness (how one sees, feels and perceives their environment as well as their internal state and triggers) in order to mindfully select the specific stimuli with which to respond to. This finding suggests that being more fully aware of one's internal state and surroundings could encourage acting with awareness of consequences, lessening one's potentiality for acting rashly when it comes to drinking. Potentially, responding to emotional stimuli as a reaction to intoxication, and thinking through potential consequences, could reduce one's desire to act on those stimuli or make risky decisions.

In Mediational Model 2 (Acting with Awareness mediating relationship between Lack of Premeditation and Drinking Consequences) the mindfulness variable was a full mediator for the pathway. Acting with Awareness entails being

45 fully present in the moment, all attention focused on one's current activity. This

finding suggests being fully present could lower the tendency of a subject to act without consideration of potential consequences, related to drinking. One way this could look is perhaps the more one is focused on their current activity, living mindfully and presently in-the-now, the more present one is with their immediate circumstances, leading to a reduction in rash acting and substance use to subdue unwanted emotions. This finding is supported through Peters et al. (2011) who found the acting with awareness facet of the FFMQ to have the strongest inverse correlation with impulsivity. Royuela-Colomer et al. (2021) also found acting with awareness to be reflected in less impulsive adolescents. Bowen and Enkema (2014) found the greater one scores in the 'acting with awareness' domain, the lower the severity of their substance dependence, as they were found to be inversely related. Hoyer and Correia (2020) and Karyadi et al. (2014) also found acting with awareness to be linked to fewer alcohol related behaviors and consequences. Lu and Huffman's (2017) study strongly upheld a substantial relationship between AA [attentional awareness] and the lack of premeditation domain of impulsivity.

In Mediational Model 3 (Nonreactivity mediating relationship between Lack of

Premeditation and Drinking Consequences), the mindfulness variable acted as a full mediator for the relationship between impulsivity and drinking. Nonreactivity is allowing thoughts or feelings to come and go, noticing but not responding to internal stimuli, and minimizing reactions towards them. In regards to drinking and acting rashly, this suggests an individual who is less likely to get caught up in their emotions and reach for a quick solution towards satiation of negative stimuli, would also be less likely to act without regard to consequences. This finding is supported

46 by literature; Gallo et al. (2021) specifically explored the association between Lack

of

Premeditation and Nonreactivity and found them related. The researchers posited

that "the greater reactivity to internal stimuli and a decreased ability to plan and

consider the consequences prior to acting would be inversely correlated" (Gallo et

al., 2021, p. 4). Both Peters et al. (2011) and Murphy and MacKillop (2012) found

Lack of Premeditation to be significantly, moderately and negatively associated

with Nonreactivity. Karyadi et al. (2014) as well found dispositional mindfulness

measures to be related to decreased substance use behaviors, particularly in the

domain of Nonreactivity.

In Mediational Model 4 (Nonjudging mediating relationship between Lack of

Premeditation and Drinking Consequences) the mindfulness variable was a full

mediator for the pathway. Nonjudging inner experience relates to the experience of

awareness of one's inner thoughts and feelings without passing criticism over them.

This could look like avoiding the

"should's" as in "I shouldn't have had another drink" or another way of

internalizing self-doubt and blame. Nonjudging would look like "I've had what I've

had but that does not imply I need to have another." This finding suggests that those

who have tools to avoid self-judgmental thoughts could have stronger resiliency

against acting rashly without considering long-term consequences. Cavicchioli

found the use of non-judging, acceptance-based ideas in mindfulness interventions

to be a protective factor for difficulty with emotion regulation effects for individuals

with AUD (2019). Hoyer and Correia (2020) also found that accepting without

judgment significantly reduced the relationship between negative urgency and drinking, and generally the use of alcohol as a coping tool. Reynolds et al. (2015)

also found inverse relations between accepting without judgment and drinking to

cope among college students. Bowen and Enkema (2014) found

Nonjudging to be a crucial domain in the reduction of severity of substance
dependence.

In Mediational Model 5 (Observing mediating relationship between Lack of

Perseverance and Drinking Consequences), the mindfulness variable acted as a partial

mediator for the relationship between impulsivity and drinking. Lack of Perseverance

entails the tendency to quit when a task becomes too challenging or mentally taxing

for the individual. In terms of drinking behaviors, this may present as a barrier

towards one's abstinence or moderation goals, or otherwise encourage disengagement

from the complexities of goal-driven behavior. This finding suggests observing,

utilizing purposeful sensory awareness of internal and external stimuli, could

encourage greater self-discipline and cognitive engagement with goals in regards to

drinking. A partial mediation implies that the skill of Observing is only one factor

that could contribute towards the relationship between cognitively disengaging with

difficult tasks and consequences from drinking. In this case, the mindfulness facet

alone did not completely negate the risk associated with impulsivity. It could still be

used as a tool in the toolbox, in assistance with other interventions targeting this

relationship between variables. The 'observing' domain is less supported by research

(beyond Murphy & MacKillop [2012] finding it positively correlated with Sensation

Seeking), so it is a relative novelty of this study. Minhas et al. (2021) found the 'Lack

of Perseverance' domain of impulsivity to have significant correlations with the

increase of alcohol misuse.

In Mediational Model 6 (Acting with Awareness mediating relationship between Lack of Perseverance and Drinking Consequences) the mindfulness variable was a full mediator for the pathway. The finding suggested that intentional focus and attention towards one present could lead towards greater resiliency against cognitively disengaging when goal-directed behavior becomes overwhelming. In drinking interventions, this can be seen in the frequent utilization of the common recovery refrain of "one day at a time", utilization of present-focus in order to help keep up one's resiliency against disengagement with overwhelming situations. In the literature, Murphy and MacKillop (2012) and Peters et al. (2011) both found a strong inverse association between Lack of Perseverance and Acting with Awareness. Vinci et al. (2016) found that individuals who endorsed problematic alcohol use were less likely to endorse certain facets of mindfulness (specifically Acting with Awareness, Nonreactivity, and Nonjudgment), indicating that they do not engage in these mindfulness practices. Hoyer and Correia (2020) agreed, finding acting with awareness linked to fewer alcohol related consequences.

In Mediational Model 7 (Nonjudging mediating relationship between Lack of Perseverance and Drinking Consequences) the mindfulness variable was a full mediator for the pathway. This finding suggests refraining from criticism of internal experience could be helpful towards reducing one's tendency to quit in boring or difficult tasks. This finding is supported by the literature. Hoyer and Correia (2020) found the mindfulness skill of accepting without judgment ('nonjudgment' domain) as a significant moderator in their study, between negative urgency and coping motives. They posited that, "As individuals were better able to allow thoughts, situations, and emotions to occur without being impacted by their immediate

49   evaluations, the link between negative urgency and coping motives became weaker"

(2020).

However, Murphy & MacKillop (2012) found Lack of Perseverance to have a weak association with Nonjudging. This is contradicted by Peters et al. (2011) who found lack of perseverance to be the most consistently associated with FFMQ scales, specifically with a significant correlation to the Nonjudging facet. This conflict of findings in the literature could be a call for more research, as a meta-analysis can aggregate the studies in order to provide better clarification and direction for scientific inquiry moving forward.

In Mediational Model 8 (Nonreactivity mediating relationship between Lack of Perseverance and Drinking Consequences) the mindfulness variable was a partial mediator for the pathway. This means that Nonreactivity is only one factor contributing towards lowered Drinking related Consequences, and mindfulness alone did not completely negate the risk associated with impulsivity. Detachment and disengagement from potentially triggering stimuli could be one tool towards resiliency against one's tendency to quit, though it would need to be assisted by other interventions to lower drinking related consequences. This mixed result is supported by literature; Murphy and MacKillop (2012) found Lack of Perseverance to have a weak association with Nonreactivity, and Vinci et al. (2016) found that decreases in the impulsivity facet of (lack of) Perseverance after a mindfulness intervention was associated only with increased Positive Affect.

Clinical Implications

Mindfulness is a crucial part of acceptance and commitment therapies (ACT), Mindfulness-Based Stress Reduction (MBSR), dialectic behavior therapy (DBT), and

50   other modalities that seek to benefit from its present-moment focus and inherent

defusion principles. ACT is a third-wave CBT that as a therapeutic modality seeks

for participants to cultivate greater psychological flexibility towards a more valued

life (S. C. Hayes, 2019). Mindfulness is one of the tools used to accomplish these

aims. One study, Bowers et al. (2021), found through the delivery of 4 ACT

workshops that overall FFMQ total scores significantly increased suggesting greater

self-rated mindfulness over the course of the intervention. Further analysis found that

in the Observing and Non-reactivity domain, there was significant improvement.

Vidal-Bermejo et al. (2020) also found that trait mindfulness improves greatly after

ACT interventions. Caviccholi

(2019) specifically explored harnessing the five facets to explore trait

mindfulness's utility in therapeutic change. Researchers state, "(a) the self-

regulation of attention (i.e., observing, describing and acting with awareness) and

(b) acceptance attitudes (i.e., nonjudgment, nonreactivity) relating to present-

moment experiences" can act as the agent of accomplishing

therapeutic aims.

Harnessing the facets of mindfulness can also have increased outcomes

towards decreased subscales of impulsivity and decreased substance use. Specific

mindfulness-based interventions have been shown to decrease impulsivity scores

among patients with substance use disorders (Tang et al., 2015; Yaghubi et al., 2017).

Khandelwal et al. (2024) found ACT to be

"feasible, acceptable, and effective in patients with Alcohol Use Disorder". Brief

mindfulness training (i.e., 60 min of training and practice) was associated with lower

levels of alcohol-related consequences and binge drinking occurrences as well as

51   increased self-efficacy and dispositional mindfulness (Mermelstein & Garske, 2015).

These findings can be used for participants who have a default high level of state impulsivity, where their sensation-seeking may be high and they are inherently encouraged to pursue reward chemicals and novel experiences, presenting as a risk factor for drinking-related consequences. These findings show that a patient who looks for quick reward could be reacting to over-awareness of unhelpful stimuli and the satisfaction of the biomechanical stress of withdrawal. Mindfulness interventions within the facets can be specifically suited to the domain of impulsivity one is responding to, in order to help them counter those day-to-day impulsive reactions. That is the predominant mechanism within which this study could help prevent drinking related negative consequences for participants.

Mindfulness interventions, harnessing these five facets, can strengthen one's trait impulsivity and learn to think differently across situations. It is a way of reducing one's 'hijacked' PFC in addiction.

Practitioners in the realm of alcohol use disorder treatment need to explore the facets of impulsivity and mindfulness independently with their patients, in order to conceptualize an effective treatment plan. In the literature, Vinci et al. (2016) found that "the level (low versus high) and specific type of impulsivity subscale matters with regard to how a participant will respond to a mindfulness versus relaxation intervention". In their study, findings indicated that for individuals elevated on Sensation Seeking, Negative Urgency, and Positive Urgency domains of impulsivity, a brief mindfulness intervention was not successful. It increased negative affect, urge to drink and decreased positive affect. Alternatively,

52   researchers found that a brief mindfulness intervention increased positive affect in

individuals with elevated levels of

Perseverance, and therefore they would present as better candidates for these

interventions. Alternatively, Park et al. (2014) found that harm reduction

interventions would be most suitable towards individuals high in negative urgency.

Interventions need to be tailored to the individual's unique needs, and this study

indicates the differences amongst nature of associations for some of the subscales of

trait mindfulness and trait impulsivity. This is also a call for further research in order

to help better inform clinical decision-making when tailoring treatment plans and

interventions for substance misuse.

One of the most salient ways the five facets of mindfulness can be effectively

utilized to facilitate substance use reduction is to encourage coping with cravings.

Khandelwal et al. (2024) found after a series of ACT interventions, participants

were assessed and demonstrated a decrease in alcohol use and craving, as well as a

reduction in frequency of drinking/heavy drinking, relapse signs, and improved

psychological flexibility. Interventions tied specifically to the five facets can target

reduction of craving imagery and intensity, encourage the ability to let go of

thoughts, feelings and emotions so as not to get overwhelmed, and engage in

intentional contact with the present moment. These would enable one to harness a

variety of coping alternatives and reduce impulsivity, minimizing consequences for

the individual.

Assumptions and Limitations

One potential limitation was that all participants would agree on what a

'drink' and 'meditating' entails, which may vary greatly based on people's

53 perceptions. In an attempt to address this potential confusion, an easily understood

layman's definition of a standard-size drink and a definition of meditation were

included along with survey questions. An additional assumption was that

participants were attentive in their survey responses, as occasionally sustained

attention can be an issue with online formats. To address this issue, the researcher

included validity checks between instruments to assess attentiveness.

One major limitation of the study is using self-report measures without a way

to externally validate the information that participants volunteer as true. An

assumption is that participants responded openly and honestly. Still, answers might

have been subjected to an internalized social desirability bias, which can affect the

reporting of certain stigmatized behaviors, like alcohol drinking. An attempt to

address this issue is to assure the participants through informed consent procedures

that their answers remain confidential and will only be collected in aggregate.

Another limitation inherent to this research format is the correlational nature

limiting causality determination, an inherent limitation to research with a

correlational base. Additionally, this study did not contain experimental

manipulation, and as answers were provided in the participant's home environment

via online formats, confounding factors could not be accounted for.

Suggestions for Future Research

This study expanded previous research to establish the link between variables

within a general population, as prior research focused predominantly on only one

variable (mindfulness, or impulsivity, or drinking-related consequences) or was

limited in age demographic. Previous studies have assessed the relationships between

mindfulness, impulsivity, and alcohol use largely in non-clinical at-risk populations,

54   such as adolescents, young adults, and college students, or inpatient treatment

facilities for addiction recovery (Gallo et al., 2021; Hoyer & Correia, 2020; Murphy & MacKillop, 2012; Peters et al., 2011; Robinson et al., 2014). Additionally, future research might explore the mechanisms with which meditation practice directly influences mindfulness. The associations have begun to be studied in this study, but there are biomechanical as well as behavioral mechanisms of meditation to be further clarified in future research. Future research should also integrate an assessment of craving into the body of research specifically to understand state-based impacts on impulsivity and to better gauge the external validity and helpfulness of varying mindfulness approaches and facets. This can help the scientific community understand how these trait variables interact with different craving and emotional states (like anxiety and arousal).

Conclusion

This study focused on the potential of trait mindfulness to act as a mediator for trait impulsivity with regards to drinking-related behaviors. Participants were gathered via online recruitment measures and completed self-report questionnaires including demographics, a quantity and frequency measure, the Five Facets of Mindfulness Questionnaire, The UPPS Impulsive Behavior Scale and Drinking Inventory of Consequences. A total of 146 participants were included in the study. Final mediation analyses included the DrInC total score and two subscales of the UPPS (Lack of Premeditation and Lack of Perseverance), with four subscales of

the FFMQ (Observing, Nonreactivity, Acting with Awareness, and Nonjudging) acting as the mediator. Overall, most analyses established mindfulness facets as full mediators with some as partial mediators. This study contributed to a growing body of literature around the clinical utility of mindfulness, specifically how unique facets may require differing interventional models to reduce risk for negative drinking consequences. These findings suggest varying ways that facets of impulsivity can be clinically utilized in the arena of substance use reduction, by directly targeting distinct features of impulsivity.